Carla King's

Self-Publishing
Boot Camp

Guide for Authors

D0757378

Carla King's

Self-Publishing Boot Camp

Guide for Authors

How to publish, promote and sell your book
in print and every popular ebook format

- Print books, ebooks, transmedia and apps
- Online retailers, e-readers and mobile devices
- For fiction, non-fiction, full-color books and more
- With helpful checklists and project management guides

Misadventures Media

Self-Publishing Boot Camp
Guide for Indie Authors

Copyright © Misadventures Media, October 2011

ISBN 978-0-9646445-3-3

All rights reserved. First published in the United States of America.

No part of this book shall be reproduced or transmitted in any form by any means, electronic or mechanical, including photocopying and recording, or by any information storage and retrieval system, except as may be expressly permitted by the publisher. The scanning, uploading and distribution of this book on the internet or by other means without permission of the publisher is illegal and punishable by law. Please purchase only authorized electronic editions. Your support of the artist's rights is appreciated.

Make requests for permission via email to:

Misadventures Media
E-mail: info@SelfPubBootCamp.com
Web: www.SelfPubBootCamp.com

SERVICES FOR READERS

Self-Publishing Boot Camp offers special discounts and supplemental materials for publishing organizations, universities, business schools and corporate training. Contact info@SelfPubBootCamp.com.

Free tips and information
To receive our free Self-Publishing Boot Camp email newsletter, sign up at SelfPubBootCamp.com

Acknowledgements

Thank you to everyone who helped with information and support through the development of this book, especially Lisa Alpine, who co-founded the Self-Publishing Boot Camp educational program with me two years ago. Many thanks to my sister Celia Kilsby, my mother Cynthia King, and my father Frank King for reading, editing, and keeping me aware of the beginner's mind. Thank you to all my "go to" pros in the industry for the time you've spent with me discussing your areas of expertise: Joel Friedlander, The Book Designer; Lyn Bishop of Zama Design; Mark Petrakis, the SEO expert; both Laurie McLean and Karen Leland for social media marketing and promotion; Ted Weinstein for the agent and publisher perspective; and Walter Hardy for website development. I also thank Mark Glaser for inviting me to express my views on self-publishing on the PBS MediaShift web channel; the feedback from publishing professionals and authors there has been invaluable. And everyone who has presented at a Self-Publishing Boot Camp workshop, thank you. I hope you'll continue to participate. Finally I want to thank you, the reader, for your input on the previous books via the website, Facebook, and Twitter. Your comments are always welcome and I look forward to hearing more from you.

About the Author

Carla King co-founded the Self-Publishing Boot Camp program of books, workshops, and seminars in 2010, and is the PBS MediaShift contributor on self-publishing. She wrote this book because people kept asking her how to self-publish. Having worked as a technical writer since 1983, she thought nothing of putting together a small bicycle guide to the backroads of the French Riviera while she lived there in 1994, and has continued self-publishing books and magazines ever since. In 1995 Carla combined her passions for travel, writing and technology by pioneering the art of the realtime internet travelogue for O'Reilly and Associates and America Online. Her book *American Borders* was developed from the dispatches that chronicle her breakdowns in small towns all around the USA on a cranky Russian motorcycle.

CarlaKing.com

SelfPubBootCamp.com

PBS MediaShift

Contents

CONTENTS

2. Clarify Your Mission and Goals 19

3. Build Your Publishing Business 25

8. Edit and Proofread   75

9. Design   83

Introduction

INTRODUCTION

Welcome to the new world of publishing possibilities. Today's technology makes it so easy to publish that anyone can realize their dream of being an author. Whether you want to write a book for your family, or you wish to attract a traditional publisher, or are setting out to start your own small press, you can start here. Today, agents, editors, and publishers even encourage authors to test their book by self-publishing.

But what is self-publishing? Traditionally, self-publishing was achieved by becoming a small business and doing it all yourself, perhaps outsourcing design, editing, formatting, website design, business, marketing, and other tasks required to create a successful book. Today, the author services companies—also known as subsidy or vanity presses, POD companies, and book packagers—have provided such easy-to-use tools and comprehensive services that the definition has expanded to include them.

There's no reason for the serious self-publisher not to use the author services companies to assist in the task of printing, distributing, and selling, but there's more to publishing than that. Editing and design, for example. Marketing and promotion. Ebooks and apps. The web and social media. Doing business as a publisher can be a rewarding challenge. Sales opportunities abound and new opportunities arrive every day.

Take advantage of all the possibilities, or choose just a few targeted channels. This book provides a step-by-step guide to the asks you need to complete from start to finish to successfully publish your book, and a solid understanding of the options open to you.

The information presented in this guide is arranged in roughly the order you need to address each step in the journey toward publishing your book. Here are those steps. Enjoy the journey!

1. Chose a publishing path

   Choose a publishing path to getting your print book and ebook into online and brick-and-mortar stores.

2. Determine your mission and goals

   Get a sanity-check on your life-work purpose and how the book fits in.

3. Take care of business

Start your business as a publisher, including creating a realistic budget, pricing, and deciding how you will sell and distribute your book.

4. Develop your brand and platform

   Why you, why now? Standing out in your genre, community and on the internet.

5. Set up your website and weblog

   Create a website and related web properties that reflects your brand and centralizes your activities for your readers and the media.

6. Set up your social media presence

   Get set-up and active on the best social media sites for your unique marketing and publicity needs.

7. Begin marketing and promotion activities

   Get yourself noticed on the web, in print, and among your peers. Here's how to do it yourself and how to outsource professionals.

8. Edit and proofread

   Focus on completing a quality end-product. Learn how to hire-out editing and proofreading.

9. Design your book

   Use graphics, photography, and typography to create an attention-grabbing look and enjoyable reading experience in both print and e-book formats.

10. Get your book into the system

Identify the information systems you need to record your book in the proper databases.

11. Make your book discoverable

How to effectively use SEO techniques and metadata to make your book rank well in search engines. It's easier than you think!

12. Format and sell your e-book

Create and sell your e-book in all the popular formats on all the popular devices in all the popular online retailers. Take your book to the next level with a multimedia-enhanced edition of your book, or even create an app based on your book for mobile devices.

13. Format and sell your print book

Print proofs, short runs, and large quantities of books using Print On Demand (POD), short run, and offset print vendors.

14. Consider a multimedia book or a book app

Might your story be adapted to a multimedia experience, or a game, or educational material available on mobile devices?

Your Publishing Path

STEP 1
CHOOSE A PUBLISHING PATH

With triple-digit growth in self-publishing services, technologies evolving weekly, and advertising hype, it's tough for authors to figure out which vendors to choose for which services. Here's how to get your print and ebook in online retailers and in brick-and-mortar stores. New options are popping up all the time, so check out the resources page online for more information.

Option 1: Using DIY tools and services to create your ebook is for authors who will create an ebook only, or well in advance of the print version. Find out how to use a DIY conversion tool or a full-service conversion house, and how to get your book aggregated to the online retailers.

Option 2: Creating both a POD book and ebook is for authors who want to create both a print book and an ebook at the same time. Here's guidance on how to choose the best combination of services to get your book formatted and distributed.

Option 3: Attracting a publishing partner is for authors who want to partner with a distributor, small press, publisher services company, book packager, or literary agent who will invest in and shepherd your book, much like a traditional publisher, in exchange for an exclusive distribution deal and significant royalty from sales.

Option 1: Using DIY tools and services to create an ebook

Here are today's most reliable ways to get your ebook created and distributed to major markets.

+ Use Smashwords and Amazon KDP (Kindle Direct Publishing) together for the widest distribution to ebook resellers.
+ Use BookBaby, because it's easier, to reach the most important ebook resellers.
+ Use a company that specializes in ebook conversion to create book files for you, then upload them yourself.

Smashwords and Amazon KDP for greatest exposure in ebook markets

An easy way to get your ebook in the market fast is to pair Smashwords with Amazon KDP. With Smashwords, your book is readable on any e-reading device, including the Amazon Kindle, the Apple iPhone/iPod Touch/iPad, the Sony Reader, the Barnes & Noble nook, personal computers, Android devices, and others. You receive 85% of the net sales proceeds from your titles (70.5% for affiliate sales), and 60% of the list price for all sales through our major retailers. (Though Smashwords makes your book available in the Kindle format, it does not distribute your to the Kindle store, so you'll need to upload it separately.)

TIPS FOR USING SMASHWORDS

— Format the MS Word doc file in compliance with Smash-words Style Guide (they have templates), or hire someone to do it for you. (Email Smashwords for a list of formatters and book cover designers.)

— Assign a unique ISBN number to the Smashwords version of your ebook.

— Join the Smashwords Premium Catalog and agree to all the contracts.

— Submit the document and the Smashwords "meatgrinder" will generate versions of your book in all the important to be aggregated in most of the major online retailers.

— Once your book is successfully converted, Smashwords offers it for sale immediately on their site, and then sends it to the major ebook sellers—except the Amazon Kindle store.

Smashwords also delivers your book as an individual book app to mobile device customers on Apple, Android, Windows Phone 7 and HP's WebOS.

The Amazon KDP (Kindle Direct Publishing) format (like your Smashwords format) is based on an MS Word doc file, so it's not a big job to edit it.

TIPS FOR USING AMAZON KDP

— Make a copy of the Smashwords doc.

— Assign a different ISBN number to the KDP version of your ebook.

— Make changes as required to comply with the KDP formatting guidelines.

— Alternately, if you're creating a POD print book with CreateSpace, then you can simply pay a $69 fee for a perfectly-formatted KDP file to upload to the Kindle store.

SMASHWORDS/KDP PROS AND CONS

+ By using Smashwords and Amazon KDP you reach the greatest number of ebook resellers.

+ If you're not concerned with reaching the greatest number of markets, but just want to cover the major markets, BookBaby might be an easier solution.

+ The Smashwords/KDP solution is great for simple text books in grayscale, not books with complex formatting, lots of graphics or color.

BookBaby for sales and distribution to most markets

Though using Smashwords and Amazon KDP gives you the greatest exposure, BookBaby gives you exposure to the major markets for less work. They also have a different pricing model. Instead of taking a 15% percentage of net sales of your book like Smashwords and Amazon do, BookBaby charges a $129 fee to convert and distribute your book (plus $19 per year after the second year).

In addition, BookBaby offers add-on services that may be attractive to authors of more complex books, or to authors who need more hand-holding through the ebook creation process.

Send BookBaby your MS Word doc file, or if you only have a PDF, InDesign, or Quark file, they'll convert it for $39.

BOOKBABY PROS AND CONS

- Unlike the Smashwords/Amazon solution, BookBaby is a single-stop conversion and distribution center that reaches both the Amazon Kindle store and other major resellers.
- Though your book will reach the most important retailers, Smashwords reaches more.
- If your book is in a PDF, InDesign, or Quark format, BookBaby can convert it to EPUB for a small fee.
- BookBaby offers conversion of ebooks with more complex formatting, graphics, and color.
- BookBaby offers add-on services such as book design, whereas with Smashwords and Amazon you have to outsource to your own designers.

+ You only need one ISBN number for the BookBaby version of your book, versus the Smashwords/Amazon solution, where you need two.

Ebook conversion services for best formatting and DIY distribution

Hire an ebook conversion service to ensure that you get a perfectly formatted version of your book in all the different formats. The cost for a simple book ranges from $150 to $350. The more complex your book is, the higher the cost. Find recommendations on the resources page.) Once you receive your files, you'll need to upload them to all the online retailers.

CONVERSION SERVICE PROS AND CONS

+ Heavily formatted books need a personal touch to look perfect in each ebook format.
+ Services quickly pick up trends like the Apple iPad fixed layout format, so that your book can be offered early in the market on devices that can read it.
+ You must manage your relationships with each ebook retailer individually, uploading to each store, agreeing to terms, and entering metadata, banking information, and other data.
+ You should assign a unique ISBN to each format (EPUB, Kindle, iPad fixed layout, app).
+ It's more expensive, but less conversion work for you.
+ You'll need to upload the proper format directly to each online retailer.

Option 2: Creating both a POD book and ebook

There are several options available to authors who want to create both a POD and ebook.

+ CreateSpace and Smashwords
+ Other POD and ebook vendors
+ A note for authors of full-color books
+ A note about Lightning Source
+ A note about subsidy and vanity presses

CreateSpace and Smashwords

Use CreateSpace and Smashwords to reach the greatest majority of ebook and print book resellers. (Smashwords is described in the previous section on ebooks. They do not print books.) CreateSpace is an author services company owned by Amazon. They offer what many believe to be the easiest, cheapest, and most thorough solution for self-publishers for both trade paperback and color books.

USING CREATESPACE AND SMASHWORDS TOGETHER

— Create your POD book using CreateSpace templates. Or, if you or your designer has created your book using another application (such as InDesign), upload the PDF files for the interior and cover.

— Keep the book private, order a copy, and if you don't like it, experiment! Edit the cover, change the fonts, make revisions and corrections. Upload the book again, order another copy, and proof it once more. This is the magic of POD. You can repeat this process as many times as you like until you are happy with your book.

— Sign up for the Pro Plan and Expanded Distribution Channel (EDC) to take advantage of CreateSpace's vast print book distribution network.

— With the EDC your book will be visible to bookstore and other distribution databases. (However, because they have a no returns program, brick-and-mortar bookstores are unlikely to stock your book.)

— By signing up with Pro Plan and EDC you get a better royalty per book on Amazon sales.

— But you get better profits elsewhere by printing and distributing with Lightning Source. (If you do this, to avoid cross-channel selling, disable distribution to other bookstores and online retailers in the Sales Channel for your CreateSpace title. Of course, if you go this route, you need to set up your book with three vendors: Smashwords, CreateSpace and Lightning Source. Profit-driven authors like this, but most authors find it easier not to.)

— Finally, when your book is perfect, pay CreateSpace $69 to create a KDP-formatted ebook file. Then, upload it to the Kindle store. (If you want to reach other ebook retailers, use Smashwords or a conversion service to create EPUB and other formats.)

CREATESPACE/SMASHWORDS PROS AND CONS

+ You get both POD and Kindle ebook formats easily and cheaply.
+ Your book will be immediately available in the Amazon store, the largest bookstore in the world.
+ Your book has global visibility to retailers via the EDC.

+ But since they don't have a returns program, brick-and-mortar booksellers are unlikely to stock your book.
+ You need to create the EPUB and other formats separately.

Other POD and ebook vendors

There are other perfectly fine services, but the ones mentioned above are the most popular and comprehensive. BookBrewer and FeedBrewer charge upfront fees starting at $19.99, and 5% of net profits when your book is sold to online retailers. Their service is unique in that you can upload content from a blog or website and then edit or rearrange the document into final form. They also launched an "ePub-to-Print" solution for $60 that generates a POD book from the EPUB file.

PubIt is an EPUB book creation service owned by Barnes & Noble that will also get your book into EPUB format. They distribute to BN.com for the Nook, iPad, iPhone, Android, and PC. However, customers can only buy your book in the Barnes & Noble store and your royalty is 40% to 60% of the list price.

A note for authors of full-color books

Authors of full-color books have fewer options because the on-demand, digital printing presses that POD companies use do not result in the perfect-quality color separation that offset printers offer, and running color books one at a time, on-demand (POD), can be prohibitively expensive.

CreateSpace has reasonable prices and fairly good color results, but Blurb is a much higher end—and higher priced—color POD vendor. Both of these vendors, as well as Lulu and others, allow authors and artists with no experience in InDesign to create a book. That's great for small-run books, family books, or portfolios, but authors who want their books to compete in the general marketplace will probably choose a path more like this:

TIPS FOR AUTHORS OF FULL-COLOR BOOKS

— Hire a designer to create the book in InDesign.

— Upload a PDF to a vendor like CreateSpace or Blurb to print proofs, make corrections, and tinker with the design until the book is perfect.

— Find a print broker to hire an offset printer (often located in Asia) to print a quantity of books.

— Order a proof from the printer, to make sure that the color is perfect.

— Order the printed books.

— Create a PDF ebook version of the book that looks exactly like the print book, minus the blank pages.

— Optionally, get the book converted to the iPad fixed layout format, an EPUB extension that uses CSS to make the book content flow beautifully inside the iPad.

A note about Lightning Source

If you've been studying self-publishing you've probably heard about Lightning Source (LSI), a publisher services company with an extremely far-reaching print book distribution network. They're owned by Ingram Content Group, so your print book will be listed with the majority of online retailers and brick-and-mortar bookstores worldwide.

TIPS FOR WORKING WITH LSI

— Sign up for an account. A sales rep will call.

— Fill out all their online forms. Sign all of their contracts and other paperwork you need for distribution to each channel and each geographical location (USA, Canada, Europe, Australia, etc.).

— Upload the PDF cover and interior files for your print book. They provide detailed specifications, including a spine-width calculator and barcode generator. Get proofs.

— Upload PDF files for your ebook.

PROS AND CONS

✦ LSI is overkill for most self-publishers, but if you're an author with more than one book and plan to become a small press, you will benefit from working with them to get books into stores overseas.

✦ LSI has the widest distribution to brick-and-mortar bookstores and online retailers who sell print books.

✦ However, instead of working with LSI directly, you can get Ingram/LSI distribution to online retailers through CreateSpace. But your book is unlikely to be stocked in bookstores, which has become the least effective sales channel for most authors, anyway.

+ If you really want to be in bookstores, LSI has a returns program, so bookstores are more likely to stock your book.

+ You need to be familiar with, or be willing to learn, all aspects of the publishing business—including the technical details for creating offset print books.

+ If you don't use CreateSpace to print your book, Amazon does not immediately stock it, so customers will have to wait. So even if you use LSI it's best to use CreateSpace to keep your book stocked at Amazon. Make sure you disable "CreateSpace Direct" in the Expanded Distribution Channel area though, so they don't deliver anywhere except Amazon.

A note about subsidy/vanity presses

POD companies are also called subsidy or vanity presses and they will print and distribute anyone's book. They offer varying levels of services at widely varying prices. Lulu and CreateSpace let you upload your book for free for sale in their stores. (They make their money from adding a percentage to the print price of each book that's sold, and they also offer add-on services like editing and design.) Author House, iUniverse, Xlibris, and others have basic to deluxe packages that can cost more than ten thousand dollars, and include all aspects of book development—editing, design, marketing, ebook conversion, and distribution. This means that you don't have to outsource all these tasks yourself, but you have little control over who is handling these tasks.

PROS AND CONS

- They do everything for you - editing, design, ebook conversion, distribution and sales.
- You have little control over who is handling these tasks.
- If you decide to leave the company, it's a hassle to get control of your book ISBN number so that distribution channels know where to buy it.
- It's a very very easy way to get your book done and in the marketplace.

Option 3: Attracting a publishing partner

The demise of traditional publishing has had a negative effect on many people in the industry, so they are scrambling to find ways to take advantage of the rise in self-publishing. Book distributors, printing companies, small presses, packagers, and even literary agents are creating services for self-publishers to sustain their business.

Key here is that most publishing partners need to believe in your book before they invest the time and effort, so you may need to woo them with a book proposal and business plan. Categories of publishing services you may want to consider are discussed here.

- Distributors
- Book packagers
- Printing companies
- Small presses
- Literary agents

Working with a distributor

Traditional distribution companies are becoming eager to work with self-publishers. One example is Small Press United (SPU), a branch of Independent Publishers Group. If you're one of the fewer than 20% accepted into their program they will present your book to resellers next to offerings from the mainstream press. They can also print your book on-demand and format your ebook.

Don't overlook the smaller distribution companies, some of whom may have very narrow specialties—for example, companies sponsored by a library who reach out to seniors writing literary non-fiction. Another might specialize in spiritual titles, or romance, or nature books. These are easier to find if you're a member of a small publishers organization, which not only have lists, but authors who can recommend them.

Working with a book packager

Another more popular option, because they accept more authors into their program, are companies like BookMasters along with their distribution partner, Atlas Books.

PROS AND CONS

+ You write the book and they handle everything else, perhaps for a fee. That's everything except marketing and promotion: printing, ebook formatting, fulfillment, and distribution.
+ The fees can really pile up!
+ Most insist on an exclusive distribution contract. That means that you buy your own books from them

(at a discount) when you want a quantity to sell on your own website or for an event.

+ Authors who do not expect to make money on their book, but are using a book to generate more customers, speaking engagements, media attention, or expertise in an industry, are attracted to this solution.

Working with a printing company

Also look for established printing companies starting to offer a wide array of publishing services, including editing and design.

Working with a small press

Many small presses are now offering co- or partner-publishing deals to authors with books that match up with their catalogues. Of course, they only take books they think they can sell, because they will edit, design, convert to ebook formats, and sometimes even aggressively market your book.

PROS AND CONS

+ You write, they publish.

+ They may handle tasks (edit, design, conversion), some for free, some for fee.

+ They will only co-publish books they believe will sell. They are interested in making a profit from your book, which means you will also profit.

+ They will probably insist on an exclusive distribution contract.

+ As in the traditional distribution options above, you make less money per book.

Working with a literary agent

Agents are finding it more and more difficult to sell good books to traditional publishing companies, so many are offering independent publishing services to authors they have represented, and to new authors they believe in. Do choose your agents carefully, study each agent's submission requirements, write a great query letter, and be ready to follow up with a book proposal.

PROS AND CONS

- Agents take a big cut of your profit margin.
- But they only make money when you make money.
- You need to write detailed book proposal.
- If they take you on as a client they believe in you.
- Agents have access to quality book production, publicity, and many other services you probably don't know about.
- They can negotiate a contract with a traditional publisher, if you choose to go that route.
- You could get very wide distribution... with the right agent.

Clarify Your Mission and Goals

STEP 2
CLARIFY YOUR MISSION AND GOALS

Set the stage for all the work to be done by stating your mission, forming a set of goals around your book, and composing a tantalizing elevator speech so that you can convey those goals to others.

1. Create your mission statement

2. Form a set of goals for your book

3. Compose your elevator speech

1. Create Your Mission Statement

Articulate your mission. Whenever you have to make a decision you can return to this mission statement to help determine if the action you are about to take serves it. You may be tempted to skip this step and just blindly jump into publishing your book, but think it out, write it down—now.

TIPS FOR CREATING YOUR MISSION STATEMENT

— Create a Mission and Goals worksheet.

— Record your mission statement and edit it as it changes. For example, why are you writing this book? Is your mission to change the world, to make money, to support your business, to leave a family legacy?

2. Form a set of goals for your book

Once you have articulated your mission, you are ready to drill down and define specific goals for your book. Goal-setting helps set the deadlines we all need to get motivated.

Your goal may be to address a small audience—family or community—or a larger audience in a geographic area, profession, lifestyle, or interest group. Maybe you are writing to establish yourself as an expert in your field, or to promote other products and services you offer. (Do you envision spinoff DVDs, workshops, a line of gourmet cookware?) Perhaps you are shooting for an international bestseller—it has been known to happen!

Perhaps you are among the many traditionally published authors disillusioned with the industry who are turning to self-publishing and creating your own small press. Or will you use your book as part of a book proposal to try to attract an agent and publisher?

TIPS FOR CLARIFYING YOUR GOALS

— Use your Mission and Goals worksheet to state both short- and long-term goals for your book.

— Edit your goals as they evolve through the process of publishing your book.

3. Compose your elevator speech

Now that you've stated your mission and set your goals, you are ready to drill down even more and create your elevator speech.

An elevator speech (or "pitch") is short enough to be delivered during an elevator ride; about thirty seconds and about 100 words. A great elevator speech makes the listener eager to hear more, and ideally results in the exchange of business cards and an appointment, or a run to the bookstore to buy your book, or a speaking engagement, or any number of other wonderful things.

If your elevator speech is good enough, people will remember it and unconsciously use it themselves when introducing you at a cocktail party or literary salon. Elevator speeches are great fodder for all kinds of things when you are marketing your book, from a radio interviewer's introduction to the back cover copy on your book.

The descriptions you use in your elevator speech may become part of your back-of-book copy, your bio, and promo materials.

It doesn't pay to be shy when writing your elevator speech. So be bold, practice, and refine until you've got it right.

TIPS FOR WRITING YOUR ELEVATOR SPEECH

— Write your elevator speech in your Mission and Goals document.

— Practice it on everyone you meet.

— Keep it handy to make sure it matches the information on your website, your bio, your book description, and promotional materials.

— Keep it updated!

Build Your Publishing Business

STEP 3
BUILD YOUR PUBLISHING BUSINESS

Self-publishers wear many hats, including that of a small business owner. This role is rewarding for many authors once they realize how much more control they have over their book and related products and services than if they had sold it to a publishing company. Here are the essentials of a book-publishing small business to get your first self-published book out the door.

1. Choose a publisher name
2. Get a DBA (Doing Business As)
3. Design a company logo
4. Outline a budget
5. Develop a business plan
6. Sell and distribute your books

1. Choose a publisher name

Choose a name for your publishing house. Keep your mission statement and goals in mind so you can be sure to choose one that fits. Think ahead, and choose a name suitable for future books, products, and services. Resist the impulse to use a family nickname, or the name of your cat. Your publisher name shouldn't scream "self-published!" but it doesn't need to sound stodgy or corporate, either. Get input from your friends, family, colleagues, members of your writing groups, and anyone else whose opinion you value.

TIPS FOR CHOOSING A PUBLISHER NAME

— Jot down some ideas for a publisher name.
— Do a web search to make sure it isn't taken.
— Create a short list by polling friends, family, and colleagues.

2. Get a DBA (Doing Business As)

In order to cash checks made out to your company name you will need a DBA, which is also called a fictitious business name. It is a simple process, but it can take up to six weeks to complete since it requires doing a search to make sure nobody else has the name. Then you have to advertise in a newspaper to announce your DBA. There's no need to use expensive online services, it's a simple procedure.

TASKS FOR GETTING A DBA

— Get DBA forms and procedures from your local city hall.

— Fill out all the forms, advertise your DBA in a local newspaper, and follow all the instructions specific to your locale.

— Take your DBA paperwork to the bank to open a business account.

3. Design a company logo

A logo is an essential element of your media presence. Use it long enough and people will begin to recognize and trust it. It is important to develop a logo that is simple and effective in various sizes. It should look great both in color and grayscale. The logo can have the company (publishing house) name integrated into it, or it can be a standalone graphic or type treatment. Because it is such an important element of any company, it is essential to enlist the services of a designer who understands your business, your mission and goals, and who has specialized in logo design. Keep in mind that this can be one of the more expensive items in your budget.

TIPS FOR DESIGNING A LOGO

— At a library or bookstore, note which publisher logos are effective on both cover and spine, and why.

— Sketch out some ideas for your publisher logo.

— Get recommendations for a designer. (See the resources page.)

— Ask for quotes. Include work to be done for both print and ebook versions.

4. Outline a budget

Creating a realistic budget is important. What can you afford to invest toward writing your book? What are your financial goals for the book? Will you support the book or will it support you? Decisions here will be helped by the statements you made in Chapter 2: Clarify Your Mission and Goals. Here's a starter list of budget items.

BUDGET ITEM CHECKLIST

— Software and hardware

— Domain name purchases

— Web hosting services

— Mailing list management

— Blogs

— Other web-based tools

— PayPal business account

— Shopping cart

— Photography

— Image and graphics

— Editing and proofreading

— DBAs

— Bank fees

— POD printing

— Offset printing

— Ebook conversion

— Bowker: ISBNs, bar codes, and SAN numbers

— Book design

— Logo design

— Office supplies

— Travel expenses

— Telephone and DSL/cable expenses

— Memberships (writers' and publishers' organizations)

— Contest entries

— Dues and subscriptions

— Advertising

— Promotional materials

— PR services

— Vendor fees

5. Develop a business plan

Merge your mission and goals statement into a formal business plan to which you can refer when guiding the direction of your publishing business in the short and long term. If you are a one-book author your business plan might consist of one simple document. If you are planning many books, or your book is tied to a product or service, it will necessarily be more complicated. There are many business plan templates on the web and in books that help. See the resources page for good business plan templates and workbooks.

TASKS FOR CREATING A BUSINESS PLAN

— Refer to your mission and goals to help keep the business plan realistic.

— Create a formal business plan complete with financial and marketing data.

6. Sell and distribute your books

Sales and distribution is a long, fluid, and creative process. It can sometimes take years for a book to take off, so set up good channels, good relationships, and good communities, and persist in marketing. Look to Chapter 1: Choose a Publishing Path for key decisions. Here's an outline of how the sales and distribution process might work:

+ Selling options

+ Pricing your book

+ Where to sell?

+ Setting expectations

Selling options

Pre-selling: If you have a store on your website you can begin pre-selling whenever you like, and you keep the profits (minus shipping and the PayPal store merchant account fee).

Mailing books: Books fit nicely in a free USPS Priority Mail envelope, and a stamp costs less than $5. (You can charge the customer for shipping.) Customers will receive the book in two days, which makes them very happy, especially during the holidays, and especially if it's autographed. Do send your books priority or first-class mail. The drastically lower cost of media mail might be tempting, but it can take a very long time to deliver, and sometimes—especially during the holidays— your book is likely to arrive to the customer later than they want and also damaged.

Subsidy presses: If you choose to create your book through a subsidy press (aka POD or author services company), they will handle sales and distribution for you and will dictate the terms. (See Chapter 13 on printing, and Chapter 12 on ebooks for more details.) You can buy books from them to sell at events, but of course it's not as profitable as with short-run or offset print services. (Independent Publisher magazine maintains an index of publishing services companies.)

Direct sales: If you sell direct to retailers, such as to stores in your area, you can negotiate their discount, but 40% to 50% is standard. You may be asked to sell on consignment, which means you won't be paid until the books are sold.

Back-of-room sales: If you are a speaker and sell direct via back-of-room sales, you get 100% of profits. At some events you may be asked to pay a small percentage to the organization or directly to the cashier who is handling the sales.

Specialty distribution: It's also possible to sell through specialty distributors—for example, someone who travels to conferences and sells books for you, or the owner of a website that specializes in your topic. They might ask for 50% to 55%. Remember, all is negotiable!

Ebook sales: Ebook sales are handled much the same. The discount is dictated by the sales channel, such as Smashwords or Amazon. You can sell ebooks directly from your own store if you have set up digital downloads. (See Chapter 5 on websites.)

Pricing your book

You may be tempted to calculate the price of your book based on what it cost to produce it. That doesn't work; you really need to price your book in line with the competition. Ebook prices are all over the place, but becoming standardized at 20% to 25% less than the least expensive print edition. $9.99 also seems to be a consumer-accepted price for ebooks.

Some marketers will tell you that to succeed, you need to price your first book free, and subsequent books at 99 cents, or $1.99 or $2.99. This may work for authors in particular genres, but it is probably not a good model for business books. Study your competition and price accordingly.

Where to sell?

You may be tempted to calculate the price of your book based on what it cost to produce it. That doesn't work; you really need to price your book in line with the competition. Ebook prices are all over the place, but becoming standardized at 20%

to 25% less than the least expensive print edition. $9.99 also seems to be a consumer-accepted price for ebooks.

Some marketers will tell you that to succeed, you need to price your first book free, and subsequent books at 99 cents, or $1.99 or $2.99. This may work for authors in particular genres, but it is probably not a good model for business books. Study your competition and price accordingly.

TIPS FOR SELLING YOUR BOOKS

— Use your website for direct sales in your online store.

— Take advantage of back-of-room sales at personal appearances.

— Make consignment deals with booksellers—brick-and-mortar and online—and retailers in your niche.

— Use Smashwords and CreateSpace to create and sell ebooks in many formats for many ebook readers, for sales and distribution in a wide array of online markets.

— Use the CreateSpace expanded distribution program to get into the Ingram database via their relationship with Lightning Source, or…

— …use Lightning Source to distribute printed books to brick-and-mortar bookstores via the Ingram book database, and your PDF-formatted ebooks to online retailers domestically and overseas.

Setting expectations

The defining fact about traditional distributors is that they vet their work, whereas POD author services companies will print and distribute almost anything. A traditional distributor will have opinions. Their reputation is on the line and they want to work with like-minded independent publishers dedicated to success. Consider them a partner.

Do not dismiss the fact that, whatever route you take, you are responsible for the marketing and promotion that will create buzz and sell your book. That is, you can't just send the books to your distributor and expect them to magically sell. (See Chapter 7: Market and Promote.) It can take years for even a very good book to rise to the top. Persistence pays off.

Develop Your
Brand & Platform

STEP 4
DEVELOP YOUR BRAND AND PLATFORM

Does your target audience know who you are? Do you interact with them? If you answered yes, then you have a platform. If you answered no, now's the time to start creating your public persona, including identifying images, graphics, words, and photographs. The ideal time to start is years in advance, but it's never too late.

Because your brand is a big part of how people perceive you in the marketplace, it's important that you present a consistent and recognizable presence and keep it for long enough that people start to recognize you. Brand and platform overlap:

* Brand can mean the feeling people have about you—the thing that you are known for. This is reflected in you writing style, your media personality, your exper-

tise or niche, and your overall image as reflected by your activities in person and in social media. This definition of brand overlaps a lot with author "platform."

+ Your brand is also made up of solid and recognizable trademark items such as your author name, your publishing house name, your photograph, your logo, colors and images—even typography on your website, social media profiles, stationery, posters, and other print materials.

Here's a path to developing your brand and platform.

1. Collect elements of your brand and platform
2. Create your author bios
3. Get a set of good author photos
4. Finalize your book title and subtitle

1. Collect elements of your brand and platform

Start by collecting elements of your brand and platform, keeping in mind how you want to be perceived while evaluating the brand and platforms of others in your field or genre.

TASKS FOR DEVELOPING YOUR BRAND

— Create a brand worksheet or folder on your computer.

— Use it to collect images of visual brands that attract you, including:

— book covers

— websites

— company logos

— graphics

— author photos

— color schemes

— typography

— Decide on your publishing house name.

— Decide on your author name or pen name. (If there's someone else with your name, for example, will you need to use your middle initial or incorporate the word "writer" in your domain name?)

2. Create your author bios

Your biographical description is a very important asset that affirms your platform. Information you share about yourself may include your education, accomplishments, professional qualifications, awards, titles, prior publications, media appearances, location, and family information. Like an elevator speech, it needs to be pithy, to the point, and entertaining. It also needs to convey how you are uniquely qualified, talented, or fascinating enough that anyone will want to read your book.

Author bios can be used on the back of the book, your website, on other people's websites, in press and news releases, in magazine articles, advertisements, speeches, at dinners, and as introductions by interviewers. You will need several bios to apply to different media, from long to short: 250 words to

30 words for various websites and social media, and just 140 characters for Twitter.

TIPS FOR COMPOSING AN EFFECTIVE BIO

— Compose bios of 140 characters, 50 words, 100 words, 150 words, and more.

— Make sure your bios are keyword-rich, as explained in Chapter 11: Make Your Book Discoverable.

3. Get a set of good author photos

Next to your author bio will be your author headshot. Your photo will become a recognizable part of your brand and your platform, so make sure that it's fairly recent and sharply frames your head and neck, and looks good in both color and grayscale.

Do try to avoid shots with a lot of competing activity in the background, or one where you've Photoshopped out your ex. You will need to be clearly recognized, even when the photo is reduced to the size of a postage stamp, because that's about all the space some social media sites give you.

Decide what you want to convey to the reader about you in your author headshot—studiously sexy, geeky glam, adventurous, beautiful, serious, and shy are examples. Also write down the physical qualities you want to highlight—your hair, eyes, or smile. What look will attract your audience? Trustworthy (or untrustworthy)? Exciting and smart and funny? Entrepreneurial bohemian? You get the picture.

TIPS FOR GETTING A GREAT AUTHOR PHOTO

— Create a photography worksheet to clarify how you want to be portrayed in your author photo.

— Gather photos of yourself that you like.

— Hire a professional photographer.

4. Finalize your book title and subtitle

Titling is an important step toward brand recognition, but creating an attention-grabbing title can be a big challenge. Feedback from others can help a lot. Writing groups, friends, family, librarians, and employees of your local independent bookshop are all great candidates.

Then there's the subtitle. Why do you need one? Because titles—often only one or two words—cannot fully describe what your book is about. Your subtitle needs to be both catchy and clarifying. It's also important that your subtitle contain metadata keywords as described in Chapter 11: Make Your Book Discoverable.

Create a worksheet to record possibilities for your title and subtitle.

TIPS FOR FINDING THE RIGHT BOOK TITLE

— Brainstorm your title. Use any method that comes to you— writing words from your elevator speech on scraps of paper and putting them together randomly, employing dreamwork, searching databases—anything.

— Ask for input from friends, family, colleagues, on Facebook, anywhere!

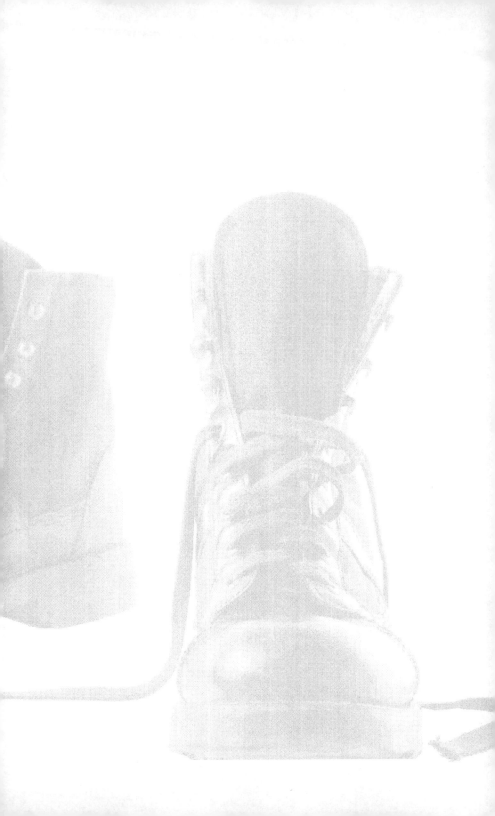

Set Up Your Website

STEP 5
SET UP YOUR WEBSITE

Your website is central to everything you do. Think of it as your storefront and your scrapbook where you collect printed materials, radio interviews, social media activities… everything. Your website should reflect your brand and it needs to be dynamic—that is, you need to update it often. Social media widgets can help, as can weblog (blog) entries, calendar entries, and updated links to articles, interviews, and other material on the web. Here's what you need to know to get your website and blog going:

1. Buy your domain names

2. Set up your website

3. Set up your blog

1. Buy your domain names

For marketing and publicity purposes, you will need a website, which means you must buy a domain name. Your domain name becomes your address on the internet that leads to your website. You should buy not only your name (and your pen name and nicknames), but the name of your book and the name of your publishing house. You can "redirect" or "forward" all those domain names to your main website, which ideally is your author name. Remember, your name is probably your strongest brand.

If your name is difficult to spell, try to buy the common misspellings as well, and forward those domains to your main site. If you have a common name, it is likely to be taken. If not, grab it now and choose .com—don't bother with .net and .org or .biz or .tv or any of the other tags if you can get a .com tag. If you cannot get a .com tag for your author name, consider adding your middle initial (http://www.carlasking.com), or use a dash or underscore (http://www.carla-king.com or http://www.carla_king.com) or even append the word "author" or "writer" to your name (http://www.carlaking-author.com). If you write for a niche market, use that description (http://www.carlakingmotorcycles.com) and if have a great nickname, use that (http://www.missadventuring.com). No matter what name you choose, use keywords on your site for maximum discoverability, so that search engines can find you by any of these names.

DOMAIN NAME SELECTION TASKS

— On a website worksheet write down all the domain names you might need, and search for their availability.

— Decide on a domain-name-hosting service, where you'll buy and manage your domain names. (Get recommendations. It helps to have a friend who knows how to navigate a domain-name-hosting service.)

— Set your main website to renew automatically so you don't lose your domain name when it expires. Better yet, buy it for the maximum number of years possible. Search engines give more weight to those who have really committed to their domain names, anyway.

— Redirect all the names you buy to a single website.

2. Set up your website

Your website is your portfolio and you need to keep it current. Unless you have the budget to keep a webmaster at your beck and call, use a system that lets you make updates yourself.

Some of your choices are: online web-builder systems (Yola), blog-based systems (WordPress, Moveable Type), do-it-yourself desktop applications (Dreamweaver, FrontPage), and web-builder tools offered by your web hosting service.

Many people prefer an all-in-one CMS solution because it keeps branding completely consistent and is simpler to manage. Others are happy with a mishmash; for example, a WordPress website and blog, Constant Contact for mailing list management and newsletters, Google Analytics for site statistics, Flickr for photos, and so on. It's a lot to keep track of.

Do some research to find a solution that's best for you. Get tips and recommendations on the resources page. Here is a checklist of features for your website.

WEBSITE FEATURES CHECKLIST

— Editable web pages: Change the words and photos on your site whenever you like using a password-protected administration from any browser.

— Blog: An integrated, fully featured blog similar to others you may have used (Blogger, Typepad, WordPress). Your readers can subscribe via an RSS feed.

— Articles publisher: Write articles or stories for publication on your site.

— Reader reviews: A form on the website lets readers type in a review of your book or product. You get notification and can edit and publish the review (or not).

— Contact form: A contact form on your website allows readers and press to directly contact you from the site. This means that you don't have to publish your email address.

— Mailing list management: Constant Contact, Vertical Response, MailChimp and other services may be integrated with your website. Readers sign up for your mailing list via a form. Bounces and bad email addresses are removed automatically. Include the URL for mailing list signup on all of your correspondence, and watch your list grow.

— Newsletter: Again, Constant Contact is an example. Make sure your newsletter is branded consistently with your website. You may have multiple mailing lists, such as one for readers and one for press releases, or any topic of your choice.

— Store: Add an integrated store (such as PayPal Pro) and earn 100% of the profits on your books and products (minus their merchant services fee). An integrated store keeps customers on your site, takes credit cards, and automates shipping and tax calculations.

— Digital document delivery: Sell ebooks, magazines, audio files, and other media in electronic format that readers can download directly from your site.

— Search Engine Optimization (SEO): Optimize your search engine placement by specifying keywords and other metadata.

— Multimedia: Upload photos, create albums, slideshows, and publish audio and video.

— Site statistics: Monitor site popularity and marketing campaign success with website statistics reports that detail users, referrers, visitor locations, and more. This may be integrated into your site or done with an add-on like Google Analytics.

— Social media features: Place a widget on your site that displays your activities on Twitter, Facebook, Scribd, and others.

It might be difficult to decide on a method and service to use to develop and maintain your website. But here are some questions to ask yourself:

— Do you have a webmaster that you trust to keep your site updated as you evolve?

— Do you want to do it yourself using tools provided by your ISP? (GoDaddy, Network Solutions, BlueHost)

— Maybe you prefer an all-in-one browser-based CMS (Yola).

— Or perhaps you are comfortable with a blog-based tool (WordPress, Moveable Type).

TASKS FOR CREATING A WEBSITE

— Research and decide on a technology/system you'll use.

— Gather materials for your pages. Browse and evaluate other author websites to gauge their effectiveness and get ideas Consider starting with these navigation items:

HOME | BOOKS | ABOUT | BLOG | STORE | NEWSLETTER |

MEDIA | READER REVIEWS | CONTACT

— Collect content like your author photo, bio, book blurb, media kit, and links to social networking sites.

— Study widgets offered by sites like Facebook, Scribd, Twitter, and Flickr, and think about how you might incorporate them into your website's pages.

3. Set up your blog

A blog is a very flexible tool. You can use it as your personal soapbox on any issue of the day, or to publish segments of your book to create excitement or ask for feedback. Since blogs allow people to respond, you can sometimes stimulate good discussions.

Your website solution might include a blog tool, but if it does not, you can display your blog entries on your website using RSS.

TASKS FOR CREATING A BLOG

— Choose a blog tool. Typepad, WordPress, Blogger, and Posterous are popular.

— Set up your account. Be sure to upload your author photo and bio, fill out your profile information, and link to your website.

— Publish your first blog entry—an introduction to yourself and what you will be blogging about. It will set the tone of all the material you will publish there. The most successful blogs stay on topic. (Remember your platform!)

Set Up Your
Social Media
Presence

STEP 6
SET UP YOUR SOCIAL MEDIA PRESENCE

Authors who are active on social media have an advantage because today's readers use social media widely to recommend books. Plus, their likes and interests are recorded and broadcast by services that help them fulfill their desires. Use social media to connect with readers, cultivate relationships with bloggers, and identify curators who can make their voices heard above the fray.

First, develop your brand and set up your website and blog so people know where to go to find out everything about you. Also, make sure you have set up a mailing list on your site so that people can sign up for your newsletters. You don't want to lose them now!

Start developing your social media presence long before your book is finished. Twitter and Facebook are popular with many authors because they're easy to use, enjoy large audiences, and provide one-click connectivity to and from many other social media sites. Some authors participate in forums, social bookmarking, and photo-sharing sites, too. Here's what you need to do now.

1. Set up your Twitter account

2. Set up your Facebook account

3. Establish your social publishing presence

4. Join and contribute to forums or groups

5. Evaluate other social media tools

6. Contribute articles and stories for publicity

7. Streamline your social media activities

1. Set up your Twitter account

Twitter is a micro-blogging tool limited to 140 characters. Use it to send out bursts of fabulously interesting information... on your topic. Include links to your blog, articles, interviews, and related information from other people. Your Twitter name should be your actual name, not a cute nickname, unless it is in line with your topic and people know you by that "handle.

TWITTER TIPS

— Register for a Twitter account. See their how-to documentation on the web. Use your own name if possible.

— Use a Twitter app that lets you know when people mention you. HootSuite is a browser-based tool and TweetDeck is a desktop and mobile application. These tools also let you time your tweets and automatically shorten URLs.

— Upload your bio and author photo to the profile page. Make sure to link to your website.

2. Set up your Facebook account

Some people use Facebook to communicate with groups of actual friends and family; others use it to communicate with people with whom they have something in common, even if they have never met. On Facebook you can create groups, company pages, virtual events, and an author page. Since you can feed your tweets from Twitter into Facebook automatically (and vice versa), it is not a lot of work to seem as if you are really active in both places.

FACEBOOK TASKS

— Sign up for a Facebook account. Try to use the same username you've used on all other social media.

— Create your personal page, then create your author page. You may also consider creating a company page for your publishing/media company, and perhaps even a page for each of your books.

3. Establish your social publishing presence

Scribd, WattPad, GoodReads, and Red Room are just a few of many other social publishing sites you might consider joining. Scribd lets you share documents (early chapters of your book, perhaps) on its site and to their "Float" app, or directly on your blog or website using a widget. It also sends reader comments via "scribbles" to their Twitter and Facebook pages. You can even sell your ebook from their site. Red Room is a community that connects writers and readers in the literary community. GoodReads is a book review and recommendation site. You can also use Amazon as a social site by reviewing and recommending books.

Contribute to the community, subscribe to others' blogs and writings, join groups, get inspiration and critiques, and make new friends. You may even become a better writer.

SOCIAL PUBLISHING TIPS

— Create your accounts with the same username you've used on all other social media, and be sure to fill in all the profile information, with links back to your website.

— Join one or more writer's communities online and post your work, join groups, and follow others. Start connecting.

— Be sincere. You can't be on every social media site, so carefully choose the ones you can keep up with and stay active in fewer rather than inactive on many.

4. Contribute to forums and groups

Forums and groups are probably the best place to get attention because they're so interactive. People who want to learn or to be inspired flock to them. You can become a star by sharing what you know, especially if you're an expert in the topic. You can also get ideas for blog entries, articles, publicity, and invite people to friend you on Facebook and follow you on Twitter. LinkedIn is a great place for professional groups.

FORUMS AND GROUPS TIPS

— Find and join the most popular groups and forums in your interest area or area of expertise.

— Use the same username as your other social media tools. Add your photo, your bio, and a link to your web page.

5. Evaluate other social media tools

You might consider sharing bookmarks on Delicious, news stories on Digg, or nerdy news on Slashdot. To expand your professional network, join LinkedIn. Create a private group on Ning. Use FriendFeed to combine all your social media activities for those who want to follow you.

6. Contribute articles and stories for publicity

Now that you are an author you can afford to write for free, because every piece of content you contribute is publicity that will generate book sales. Other than magazines and websites on your topic, there are many websites that host articles and stories and market their best contributors. Examples are examiner.com and howto.com. You can cross-post on your own website and social publishing sites.

ARTICLES/STORIES TIPS

— Identify parts of your manuscript that might become articles or stories, photographic layouts, or other short pieces.

— Offer free articles to magazines, newspapers, and websites in your area of expertise in exchange for a linked blurb about you and your book.

7. Streamline your social media activities

Make your social media properties work for each other. Set them up so they automatically send updates to your various other sites. Send your tweets to your Facebook wall. Send Scribd scribbles to both your Facebook wall and your Twitter feed. If you use GoodReads, or other sites, connect them, too. Sign up for FriendFeed to aggregate your feeds all in one place.

These sites make it very easy to connect with "share" buttons, the ability to log in using your Facebook credentials, and other methods. Simply follow their instructions.

TIPS FOR YOUR SOCIAL MEDIA ACTIVITIES

— Decide if you want your Twitter, Facebook and LinkedIn status to update to each other.

— Use a tool like TweetDeck to update all three (or two) at the same time.

— Consider using FriendFeed to aggregate all your updates.

— Each time you join a community, look for their "share" function and consider using it.

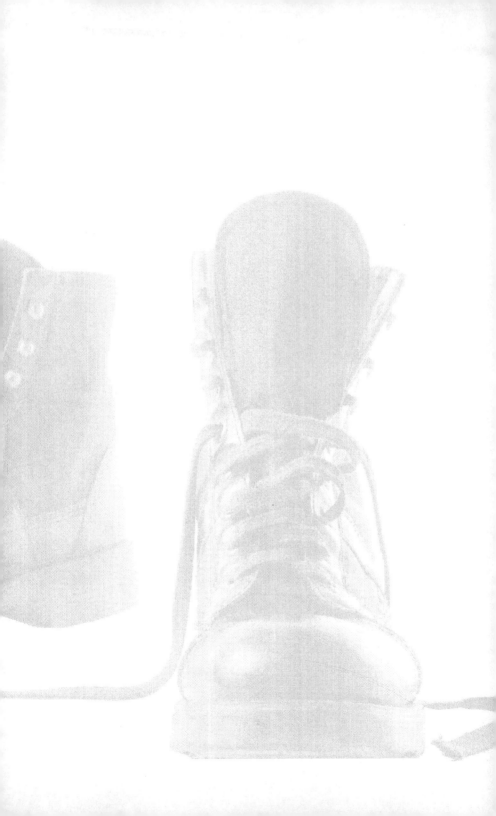

7

Market and Promote

STEP 7
MARKET AND PROMOTE

Marketing and promotion activities never end. Here's how to start, along with some ideas on how to continue the process throughout the life of your writing career.

1. Create a web marketing strategy

2. Set up your mailing list

3. Consider hiring a publicist

4. Build your online press kit

5. Write a press release and send it to the media

6. Join writers' and publishers' organizations

7. Explore trade organizations

1. Create a web marketing strategy

Ongoing promotion is absolutely essential for generating sales and for building your brand and platform. Building a social media presence should be an essential part of your week. Web promotion and social media activities generate incoming links to your website, which boosts your discoverability in search engines, which also builds your author platform.

In the traditional media world, don't be shy about contacting reporters—from podcast hosts to local news staff and even television hosts. They will call you if they need your expertise. Only you can dream up the promotional possibilities in your niche. Be creative!

Here's a starter checklist for ongoing promotion.

WEB MARKETING TASKS

— Update your website regularly with events, social media activities, interviews, and podcasts.

— Collect materials for your online press room for the media. Include assets like high-resolution photos of you and your book covers.

— Tweet, blog, use Facebook, join forums, and participate in as much social media activity as you can maintain.

— Offer a free sample chapter to your followers, mailing lists members, friends, and to readers of articles you publish.

Include a discount code that's different for each market, so you can track the effectiveness of each venue.

— Write monthly newsletters to the people who have signed up for your mailing list.

— Contribute stories to as many print and online publications as you can, and include bio and book order information.

— Create a news release when news happens on your topic, to relate you and your book to current events.

MEDIA CONTACT TASKS

— Scan Help A Reporter Out (HARO) for media opportunities.

— Pay for a targeted media list when you're ready to send a press release.

— Offer discounts or free shipping to social media friends.

— Participate in podcasts, or even start your own.

— Send copies of your book to podcasters, journalists, reviewers, interviewers, and conference organizers.

— Create audio and video clips of your readings or an interview to include on your website.

— Consider producing a book trailer to post on YouTube.

2. Set up your mailing list

Make sure you've got a way to collect the email addresses of people who are interested in you and your book. The best way to do this is through an automated system on your website. If your website is not set up with a mailing list manager and newsletter tool, you can use one of the many for-fee services like Constant Contact or Vertical Response.

MAILING LIST TASKS

— Set up your mailing list. Make sure it has the same branding—colors, logo, images, typography—as your website.

— Create a link on your web page inviting people to join your mailing list.

3. Consider hiring a publicist

For the indie author, affordable publicity is difficult to find, but not impossible. On the next page is a starter list for interviewing a potential publicist. (Check the resources page for specific recommendations.)

Nobody can guarantee which publication, blog, radio, or TV show will run with a review of an author's book or interview the author as an expert, but there are certain things a dedicated publicist can do to customize the PR campaign and improve the odds the writer will get picked up by media. The problem with the generic approach that author services companies take is that it's one-size fits all, which rarely produces the best results.

Start promotion activities as many as two years before your book is published. This builds your platform. These activities include getting a website, blogging, and taking advantage of social media and networking tools. If you're going to hire a publicist, request a detailed plan that includes the specific projects that will be part of the campaign, the timeline for delivering on these projects, what you as the author are expected to provide to the publicist, and the process by which the publicist will keep you updated on the progress of your campaign. And be sure to ask him or her to provide contact information for other authors as references.

TIPS FOR HIRING A PUBLICIST

— Research publicists in your area and nationally. Get recommendations and references.

— What do they charge? And for what, exactly? (Sending out news releases, blog tour setup, etc.)

— How do they go about it? Ask about their process and approach.

— What is their actual expertise promoting indie authors? Ask for an author list, and references.

— How well do you connect personally? Do you like each other?

— How personalized is the service?

4. Build your online press kit

Make sure your website has a press page where reporters can download high-resolution photos of your author photo and your book cover. There should also be a list with links to all the media that have already covered you. Here's a list of items that should be in your online press kit.

ONLINE PRESS KIT CHECKLIST

— High-quality author photo

— High-quality image of book cover

— Links to your bios of 25 words, 50 words, 100 words, and more

— Links to interviews with you

— Links to articles about you

— Links to articles by you

— Links to your book reviews

— A link to your events calendar

— Your contact information

5. Write a press release and send it to the media

Before you buy, carefully scrutinize any press release distribution Before you buy, carefully scrutinize any press release distribution service. Many promise distribution to national and international media outlets for less than $500, which sounds very attractive. But press releases have to be incredibly well-written, titillating, topical (automotive, gardening, etc.) or timely (tied to a major news event) to get noticed by busy journalists, and there's no guarantee it'll be picked up. It's probably best for you to handle this yourself, targeting the media you know is right for you, or to hire a publicist.

Look for a service that will give you a targeted media list based on keywords, and that will help you write a great press release and provide you with a monthly newswire service. There's a special recommendation for this kind of service on the resources page.

Think creatively. You might hire a magazine editor or well-known personality in the field you're writing about to send emails to their contacts. The email can have all the information a press release has in it, but would be crafted like a personal note.

6. Join writers' and publishers' organizations

Many writers work in isolation, so it is very healthy to get out into the larger community. Plus, it is beneficial to your ongoing promotional needs to keep up with changes in the industry, new technologies, services, and sales and distribution channels. Here are some communities you might consider.

ORGANIZATIONS YOU MIGHT JOIN

— Independent Book Publishers Association (IPBA, formerly PMA—Publishers Marketing Association)

— Small Publishers Association of North America (SPANnet) has a great member forum.

— Small Publishers, Artists and Writers Network (SPAWN)

— Local publishers' organizations and associations have the advantage of offering face-to-face meetings, opportunities, and commiseration. You may not need to be a member to attend their events. Search for "independent publishers associations" in your area.

7. Explore trade organizations

You might benefit from relationships with trade organizations related to your topic. Funded by dues, they have money and may host, sponsor, or organize conferences. They are often happy to enliven their program with an author appearance. Here are some examples of trade organizations: The Fragrance Foundation, Organic Trade Association, International Housewares Association, Motorcycle Industry Council, Adventure Travel Trade Association, and The United States Association of Professional Investigators.

The value of contacts in trade organizations related to the topic of your book, or that your fictional character specializes in, cannot be underestimated. They're large groups—a captive audience of people who want to hear more about what they do.

Edit and Proofread

STEP 8
EDIT AND PROOFREAD

Along with all your other tasks, you may still be trying to finish writing, editing, and proofreading your book. Here's where writers' groups can be a big help or, if you have the budget, a book coach. Giving your editor the best possible manuscript will save you considerable review cycles and money.

1. Consider hiring a book coach

2. Join a writing group

3. Calculate time to completion

4. Get professional editing and proofreading

5. Print proofs using a subsidy press

1. Consider hiring a book coach

Some people hire a book coach at the very beginning of their project, before they have even written a draft, to make sure that the project is viable and that they will be able to bring it to fruition. If you don't have the luxury of a budget for this task, an effective writing group can help.

TIPS FOR HIRING A BOOK COACH

— Search the web to find candidates in your area.

— Get recommendations for book coaches from writers you know.

2. Join a writing group

Writing groups come in all flavors. If you are writing a business book you won't get much help from a group of romance writers, for example. Your writers' group should consist of people who are as committed to their projects as you are to yours. They should be able to give you constructive suggestions delivered in a positive tone. How do you know a writing group is good for you? You go home energized and excited about your book. If you leave depressed and irritated, let that be the last meeting you attend. Here are some ways you might find a group.

TIPS FOR FINDING A WRITING GROUP

— Search for writing groups on the web.

— Post a notice on craigslist.org or meetup.com.

— Query local writing and publishing organizations.

— Post notices at your library and local bookstores.

3. Calculate time to completion

Create a book chapter outline and then set a regular writing schedule. Figure out how long it takes you to write the first draft of a chapter. If you keep a steady pace, you should be able to calculate how much time it will take to complete. If you workshop two chapters a month, when will your book be finished? How about four chapters a month? Calculate the number of chapters you need to workshop per month to get your book ready for professional editing and proofreading.

TIPS FOR GETTING YOUR BOOK FINISHED

— Calculate how long it will take to finish writing your book.

— Record these goals in your calendar.

— If it helps, find a writing partner or group who will help you meet those goals.

4. Get professional editing and proofreading

Professional editing makes a huge difference to your success in the general marketplace. A developmental editor makes sure the content is appropriate for your genre and readership, that the book has a narrative arc, that your chapters flow, and whether text needs to be moved or cut. Have you dropped a character or story line that leaves the reader hanging (or yawning)?

In fiction and creative non-fiction the plot, pace, dialog, and character development will be examined. In non-fiction, the editor will also analyze the effectiveness of lists, graphics, and illustrations. In photography and art books, a visual storyline will be analyzed.

The next step is line editing, also called copy editing. The editor makes a meticulous line edit to correct grammar, spelling, and punctuation. Your editor will collaborate with you to create a style sheet to follow, for consistency.

Finally, proofreading is done once a "proof" copy of the book is printed. (See Chapter 13 on printing for more information on printing proofs.) Editing and proofreading is, unfortunately, skipped by many self-published authors.

TIPS FOR FINDING THE RIGHT EDITOR

— Get recommendations from other writers and see the resources page.

— Ask for a quote. Start with one chapter to see if you are compatible. Or pay for a manuscript review before committing to a complete edit.

— Consider recruiting peers to do a peer review of your book. They may also become future reviewers from whom you can collect blurbs.

5. Print proofs using a subsidy press

Subsidy presses CreateSpace and Lulu let you upload a PDF of your book for free and order as few as one copy at a time. Using these services to proof your text, pagination, and design is a convenient and inexpensive way to print proofs.

9

Design

STEP 9
DESIGN YOUR BOOK

Designing both ebooks and print books involves creating a look for the interior and book cover, plus the spine and all the graphic elements, photography, and type treatments. Cover design is used to grab the customer's attention. Interior design is used to convey information and orient readers; they need page numbers, captions, and chapter and section titles to guide them.

Design is extremely subjective, but readability is key. Authors of text-heavy books naturally put less emphasis on design than authors of photography or children's books, who are often more willing to pay for a professional designer.

Choosing your design program is of extreme importance. Though plain text can be copied and pasted among many different tools, design elements and stylesheets cannot be exported.

If you've meticulously created paragraph styles in Microsoft Word, they'll be lost when you paste your book into InDesign, and vice versa. Automatically generated headers and footers will also be lost.

You or your designer must export your book to PDF format to print it. As long as you have a PDF file you can print it with any service. The PDF can also be offered as a digital download for reading on computers and devices. Ebook conversion services can also work with PDF files.

The material in this chapter will help you understand design tools to decide if you need a professional designer, and provides the information you need to hire someone. Here are the step:

1. Research books in your genre
2. Choose a standard book size
3. Choose interior typography, fonts, and dingbats
4. Choose paper stock
5. Calculate spine width
6. Create a detailed book specification
7. Gather the elements of your book cover
8. Choose a design service
9. Create print-ready files
10. The last important step: metadata

1. Research books in your genre

Visit Amazon, GoodReads, and other book sites, or go to bookstores and libraries to study book covers in your genre. Book buyers and readers will expect yours to fit into your category. For example, if your non-fiction book has a curlicue font, it will look like a romance novel. So don't get too creative in your attempt to stand out. Readers will be subliminally confused by deviations from genre standards. Note the following details.

BOOK DESIGN CHECKLIST

— Book size: Take a measuring tape with you. What is the most common size in your genre? (Designing a custom, non-standard book size will raise your printing costs astronomically.)

— Cover art: Are most of the books using graphics, photography, or a combination of the two?

— Cover font: Look at the typography used for book titles. Are they serif fonts with lots of curlicues (romance novels) or sans-serif fonts (non-fiction)?

— Finish: Are the covers in your genre mostly glossy or matte? Are they laminated?

— Back of book: Back-of-book text is the most effective way to attract buyers. There, they find out what the book is about, why the author is so fabulously interesting or qualified, and how many important people recommend it. Notice what is tantalizing and what is distracting, and write your copy to compete.

— Paper color, weight, sustainability: Do books similar to yours use crème or white paper? 55 or 60 lb. weight? (You might ask a librarian for help, or order samples from printers.) Ask about recycled and sustainably harvested paper.

— Interior font: Text-heavy books use serif fonts (they're easier to read) with sans-serif for titles, pagination, and front matter. If you see a font you like, you might find it named on a colophon page (production notes that describe the text typography, the book's designer, software used, printing method, the printing company, and the kind of ink, paper, and even cotton content.)

— Dingbats and graphics: How are dingbats and graphics being used? As chapter separators? Liberally? Judiciously? Do they enhance or detract?

— Create a design folder. Use Google's image search or visit Amazon.com to find book covers and interiors you like, and save them in a folder on your computer to refer to when you are ready to design your book.

2. Choose a standard book size

Choose an industry-standard book size. For example, for trade paperback, one standard size is 5.5" x 8.5" "trim" size (book size), which means that the document it's designed in needs to be specified as 5.75" x 9.

TRIM SIZE	DOC SIZE
5.5 x 8.5	5.75 x 9
6 x 9	6.25 x 9.5
7 x 10	7.25 x 10.5
8 x 10	8.25 x 10.5
8.5 x 8.5	8.75 x 9
8.5 x 11	8.75 x 11.5

3. Choose interior typography, fonts, and dingbats

There are literally thousands of typefaces to choose from. A good rule is to choose one serif font (for text) and one sans-serif font (for headings, footers, captions, etc.) You may think that's limited, but if you use a "pro" font you will have many more styles at your disposal than just italic and bold. If your book is heavy on photography or art, you may choose to treat typography as an artistic element or choose one simple font to avoid distracting the reader from the visual story. In every case, your book's type will deeply, yet subconsciously, affect the reader. Record your preferences on a worksheet.

TIPS FOR CHOOSING FONTS

— What fonts do you like? Do some research and jot down a few serif and sans-serif fonts that appeal to you and appear readable at 10-14 point size. Make sure they are in line with the books already published in your genre.

— Do you or your designer own the fonts you've chosen? (Designers usually own many fonts and font folios.) If not, buy them. Use Adobe's Font Finder and other tools on the web.

— Choose dingbats—typographical flourishes, ornaments, or characters—to provide graphic elements for separating chapter numbers from chapter titles and other uses. Here are some examples from the Adobe font "Type Embellishments." You can find many others on the web.

4. Choose paper stock

If you are printing your book with a traditional offset printer, you'll have the luxury of choosing your paper stock. If you are printing with a POD services company, you may not have a choice.

If you print with an offset press you'll learn that the elements of book design, production, and printing choices are inextricably intertwined. See Chapter 13: Create and Distribute Your Print Book, to understand the issues.

Order sample books from printers you are considering and note the following:

PAPER STOCK CHECKLIST

— Book interior paper weight

— Book cover paper weight

— PPI

— Binding

— Cost for page count

5. Calculate spine width

Book binding, cover finish, and weight (hardcover or paper-back), plus the paper weight of the book interior, all determine the width of the spine. Recycled 55 lb. paper might actually be thicker than 60 lb. non-recycled, depending on its bulk. So you will definitely need specs from your printer. It is not uncommon to print with a few different companies during the evolution of your book. For example:

TIPS FOR CALCULATING SPINE WIDTH

— You might experiment with your book design and print cheap proofs with a POD service company like CreateSpace or Lulu.

— After that, you might print a short run of 100 with a short-run printer like 48HrBooks.

— Finally, when you decide the book is perfect, you may decide to go with an offset printer for a price break on 1,000 or more.

If you do all three, you will need to create three different versions of your book cover with different spine widths that create different sizes of your book file. If your book is 5.5 x 8.5 and the spine width is .438, your book file size in InDesign, for example, will be 11.438 x 8.

Many POD services companies provide browser-based tools that let you create your book cover without having to worry about specs. Otherwise, you'll need to look for a spine width calculator on each of their websites

6. Create a detailed book specification

A book specification provides details for your book designer and offset printer. Choices are dictated by the size of your book and the printer's specification, which are standard. A sample book specification is provided on the Self-Publishing Boot Camp website Sample request for RFQ (Request for Quote) and Quote. And here is the information your offset printer will need, with sample information filled in.

BOOK SPECIFICATION SAMPLE DATA

— Quantity: 1,000; 2,500; and 5,000

— Number of Pages: 240

— Trim Size: 5.5 x 8.5

— Interior Copy: Black

— Illustrations: 24 grayscale

— Bleeds: Full (on cover)

— Paper: 100% recycled 50 lb. crème

— Ink: All black, soy

— Proofs: PDF

— Color Cover: four-color

— Binding: Perfect

— Lamination: Matte varnish full coverage

— Shrink Wrapping in 6's

— Delivery: Mac InDesign CS2 working files + laser proofs

— Shipping: address of location (residence or business)

7. Gather the elements of your book cover

Collect assets and information into folders and files (on your computer or in print) so that when you are ready to design the book, you are ahead of the curve. Here are the assets you will need for the front of your book, the back of your book, and the spine.

BOOK COVER CHECKLIST

FRONT OF BOOK

    — Title and Subtitle

    — Author

    — Background color

    — Graphics

    — Photography

    — Font choices

BACK OF BOOK

    — Author bio

    — Marketing copy

    — Testimonials

    — Background color

    — Graphics

    — Photography

    — Font choices

    — Publisher name

    — ISBN number

    — Bar code and price

— BISAC standard subject headings

SPINE

- Author name
- Book title
- Publisher name
- Publisher logo
- Font choices
- Color

8. Choose a book design service

Three common design choices by self-publishing authors are to write and publish the book in Microsoft Word themselves, or use an author services company's design services, or to hire a professional designer. The pros and cons of each method are described below. But before we start, let's look at the importance of using styles.

The importance of styles

Whatever tool you use, create styles and apply them to each and every line in your book— chapter heads, headings and subheadings, paragraphs, headers and footers, titles, subtitles, and more. You can set your chapter head style to create a page break before it, and even set it to start on the next odd page. You can create sections that include the chapter number automatically in the footer, next to the page number. You can generate an automatic table of contents, too.

The time you spend learning how to use styles is time saved and frustration avoided when you want to make changes. Instead of having to change every instance of an element, such as a chapter head, you simply change the style and all the paragraphs automatically change to match it. In fact, you might want to hire an expert to set up a template for you, or download one from the internet or use a template provided in the application. The main point here, in case you haven't noticed, is USE STYLES!

TIPS FOR APPLYING STYLES

— Create a file with margins and gutters set in the FORMAT > DOCUMENT option in MS Word, or FILE > DOCUMENT SETUP in InDesign to specify the size of book you've chosen.

— Learn about styles on the web, or buy a book.

— Apply a style to each and every paragraph in the book. Do not use tabs and hard returns to create indents. Learn how to create white space above and below each paragraph using styles.

— Consider hiring an expert to create a template for you.

Using a word processing program for design

A word processor is a very good writing tool with a fair amount of flexibility, but if you're competing in the general marketplace, remember that it won't give you nearly as professional a look as a book design tool like InDesign. (This book was created in InDesign.)

Certainly, if you're planning to simply create an ebook to upload to Smashwords and the Amazon KDP program for reading on a Kindle, you must format a Microsoft Word doc as per their instructions. And POD services supply Word templates so that you can create your printed book. But traditional publishing does not use Word for a reason, and if you intend that your book compete alongside books in the mainstream press, you shouldn't either.

Using an author services company's design services

A popular option for designing and printing a book is to use the browser-based tools supplied by a POD services company. It's conceivable that you've gotten this far and you become so tired that you just want somebody else to handle it. That's fine, as long as you know what you're giving up. There are reasons to go with a service. These companies make it very quick and easy to design and print a book.

What's the trade-off for low cost-to-entry and ease of use? Less-sophisticated design options, fewer print choices (though you can export to PDF and print elsewhere), the inability to set your own price, smaller profits and, sometimes, a lower-quality end product. Also, unless you are great at design, or they give you a good designer, the look of your book may scream "vanity press!"

Consider using an author services company to publish your book if most of these scenarios fit.

WHY USE A SUBSIDY PRESS?

— You are on a tight budget and cannot afford software or a design professional.

— You don't have design skills.

— You are really only going to write one book, perhaps for a captive audience such as family, or for business or academic use.

— Your book is for a limited audience and you are not looking to compete in the general marketplace.

— You want a quick, low-cost proof of concept and don't mind redesigning it later.

If you decide to work with an author services company, consider these factors.

WORKING WITH A SUBSIDY PRESS

— When someone buys your ISBN for you, they control your metadata. So consider buying it directly from Bowker. (See Chapter 10: Get Your Book Into the System.)

— Compare setup costs versus printing costs. (Lower setup fees may reflect higher per-book printing costs.)

— Obtain samples of books to assess print quality. (Look for covers that peel, bindings that crack.)

— Do they provide a phone number so you can talk with a rep, or can you only contact them by email?

— Can you order just one book at a reasonable cost?

Hiring a professional designer

Professional book cover designers know the market and can help your book get noticed. They also know the value of typography and how to best include essential elements like your logo, the publisher name, ISBN, and bar code. A professional book designer will use InDesign or Quark.

While author services companies have a staff of professional designers, they don't let you choose which designer you get. So if you think you are going to be very particular about this process, it's probably better to hire this out yourself.

There's a good number of cover designers (and formatters) on the Smashwords site who will design your book for a very reasonable fee.

Make sure that the designer you choose has designed books like yours, or at least is familiar with competing books, and that you get along with him or her personally. It's an intimate process.

9. Create print-ready files

Your printer or ebook distributor may require that you upload files in a specific format. Printers will want one "trouble-free PDF" for the cover and one for the interior. Or they might want one file for the interior and three different files for the cover—the front, the back, and the spine. They may or may not provide a template. So make sure you and your book designer know how to do this.

Ebook companies may want to distribute the book on readers that use the EPUB format, so you need a version of your book for that. Amazon and Smashwords want a Microsoft doc file formatted a particular way. Find recommendations for formatting services on the resources page.

10. The last important step: metadata

Before you submit your ebook for publication, you need to make sure that your document file has the correct data about you and your book in it. Even though this data is hidden to users and readers, it is used by search engines to discover your book. This is important because, for example, if you're using your friend's copy of Microsoft Word or InDesign, your friend's name is likely to be discovered as the author of the book. You can also add the title of your book and keywords to the info space in many applications. Find out more about metadata and how to make sure it's accurate in Chapter 11: Make Your Book Discoverable.

10

Get Your Book
Into the System

STEP 10
GET YOUR BOOK INTO THE SYSTEM

You want the world to know that your book is available, and the world wants to know! It's essential to successful marketing and promotion to put your book information in the book industry's databases.

1. Buy ISBNs, a SAN, and bar codes from Bowker

2. Add your title to the Books In Print database

3. Submit your book to the Copyright Office

4. Obtain a Library of Congress CIP record

1. Buy ISBNs, a SAN, and bar codes from Bowker

There's no reason you shouldn't buy your own ISBNs and it's incredibly easy. Besides, when you allow a company to provide the ISBN for your book, you give up control of the data associated with the book and you may not even be the publisher of record.

If you have let someone else buy your ISBN and print and distribute the book with their service, and then a while later decide to print your book elsewhere, customers will only see that it is no longer available. If you controlled the ISBN, you could have pointed to the second edition— a favor the company you're abandoning will rarely be willing to do.

Visit Bowker Identifier Services to purchase a block of 10 ISBNs for under $250. Why 10 and not one? Because they're a lot cheaper in bulk (a single ISBN is $125), and you need separate ISBNs for the print version of your book and each ebook format made available: Kindle, EPUB, PDF, etc. (according to the ISO 2108:2005 standard). You can also purchase EAN bar codes for each ISBN, from Bowker or another company on an as-needed basis for your print editions. (See the resources page for other bar code suppliers.)

For example, if you upload a Kindle version to Amazon via the KDP program, you must assign it a separate number from the ebook version you upload to Barnes & Noble. But if you use Smashwords to distribute your ebook, then you only need a single ISBN for the Smashwords edition of your book, even though it will be aggregated to many different readers in many different formats.

Visit the Bowker publisher page and check off these tasks as you do them.

TASK LIST FOR BUYING ISBNS

— Buy a block of 10 ISBN numbers. (You will need to assign a different ISBN to each form of your book: print book, audio book, and separately available ebooks.)

— When your book is ready to publish, fill out all the metadata in the Bowker system so that your book will be discoverable to readers and distributors. This is described in more detail in Chapter 11: Make Your Book Discoverable.

— If you plan to publish more than one book, also purchase a SAN (Standard Address Number), which is a publisher identifier. The use of the SAN significantly reduces billing errors, books shipped to the wrong points, and errors in payments and returns.

— Buy a bar code for the book(s) you are printing only when you have decided on the retail price of your book. (You cannot change it once it's assigned.) An ebook does not need a bar code unless you have designed it to be downloaded and printed to then be scanned by a bar code reader at a store. Bar codes can be purchased from Bowker or another service.

2. Add your title to the Books In Print database

The Books In Print database is managed by Bowker and supplies libraries, booksellers, publishers, and other information professionals with the details you provided about your book.

— Go to Bowker.com.

— Choose Data Services to register your title.

3. Submit your book to the Copyright Office

In the USA, the Copyright Office's eCO Online System makes it very easy to file a copyright registration for your book.

— Visit the eCO Online System and submit electronic copies of your work.

You should receive the confirmation in about four months. (Do not send a physical copy of the book; they no longer want them.)

4. Obtain a Library of Congress CIP record

You are not eligible to get a Library of Congress number for your book unless you publish five or more titles per year. Instructions are online.

Make Your Book
Discoverable

STEP 11
MAKE YOUR BOOK DISCOVERABLE

Making your book discoverable to search engines is perhaps the most important piece of your marketing strategy. After all, readers and booksellers must be able to find your book to buy your book. Key to this is search, which relies on metadata. Metadata is simply data about data, or words about words.

To search engines, all words have a value, and "keywords" have more value still. These keywords must be strategically selected and then placed where they can do the most good. Creating metadata tags is a marketing challenge that requires both editing skill and narrative common sense, two qualities that most writers possess.

People make entire careers out of SEO and metadata, but you really can do this yourself. Pay attention to how your page is ranked in search engines and look at how competing pages have gotten to the top by taking a peek at the metadata inside the metatags in their source code.

But metadata isn't the only way you get to the top of search engines. Other factors are the length of time you have owned the domain name, how active your website is, how active you are on social media sites, and the number of incoming links, to name just a few.

Metadata automates a formerly labor-intensive task by connecting readers, curators, and distributors to books more efficiently than ever before. The self-publisher who understands metadata levels the playing field to compete alongside big publishing—but only if you use it. Here's what you need to know about providing metadata about you and your book in all the relevant systems:

1. Create your keywords list
2. Create your title and description tags
3. Include metadata for images
4. Complete your Bowker record
5. Include metadata in documents and other media
6. Include metadata on reseller sites
7. Include metadata on social media sites

1. Create your keywords list

First, we must spill into search engine optimization (SEO) territory. The typical self-published author doesn't need to hire an SEO expert, but it helps to become familiar with the subject.

Try to keep the number of repeated keywords to a maximum of three. The final list should be no more than 10 to 20 words with a 900-character maximum. Then you'll have a keywords list to be used for your book metadata, for creating tags on blog posts, and in your social media activities. Create a worksheet to help you narrow down your keywords.

TIPS FOR CREATING AN EFFECTIVE KEYWORDS LIST

— Record words and short phrases you think your readers might enter into a search engine to find you and your book.

— Eliminate the less important and more generic words and phrases from your list.

— Look at the metadata in the source code of web pages of authors with competing books to see what terms they're using. In most browsers you can see it using VIEW > SOURCE in the toolbar.

2. Create your title and description tags

Most major search engines (like Google) no longer factor in the keyword metatags in search results, so this just makes having effective TITLE and DESCRIPTION tags all the more important. (Similarly, your file names should be descriptive.)

TIPS FOR CREATING TITLE AND DESCRIPTION TAGS

— Create a metadata worksheet and record the following infor— Create a metadata worksheet and record the following information:

— Draft a TITLE metatag for each separate page of your website that describes that particular page in a nutshell. Use your top keywords and make it informative first to users, and second to search engines. Set a maximum of 60 characters, including spaces.

— Finally, considering both your keywords and your TITLE, draft a succinct but keyword-rich DESCRIPTION of your book. Make this one informative to search engines first and users second. Keep it to a maximum of 150 characters, including spaces.

— Also of great importance are the actual words on each web page and, more specifically, the words used in the opening paragraphs on the page, which need to indicate exactly what that page is about.

— Be sure to use keyword-rich sentences in your opening sections. For this reason, it is wise to begin each page of your website with words and not images.

Many website creation software programs and blog services provide you with simple forms where you can enter these various metatags, which are then inserted for you into the page's HTML source code.

3. Include metadata for images

Metadata also includes the important ALT tags that offer short text descriptions for images. Here's what you need to tag:

TIP FOR ASSIGNING METADATA TO IMAGES

— Tag the image of your book cover with: ALT ="[Your book title: Book description with keywords"]

— Tag your author photo with ALT =["Your name: short, keyword-rich description of author."]

— Tag any photo on your web pages with a thorough description of the person, object, place, or other descriptive words.

You can ask your webmaster to help you do this, or, if you're using a content management system, there's probably an easy way to tag your images as you insert them into your site.

The ALT tags, like other metadata, are collected by search engines to identify and rank your pages and display them to the user.

4. Complete your Bowker record

Whoever buys your ISBN from Bowker controls the metadata for that book—so it probably should be you.

Once you've bought your ISBN, and your book is ready to publish, simply log in to your account on Bowker's identifier services page, click your ISBN number, and fill out the data in the full title detail form.

You have the opportunity to insert lots of data here—title, author, description, number of pages, size, language, copyright year, date of publication, contributors, category, title status (out-of-print, active, etc.) price, currency and a photo of your book cover. All this information is disseminated to distributors, wholesalers, libraries and retailers (online and brick-and-mortar) so they can convey it to readers. Research the BISAC standard subject headings that describe your book category and print on the back cover of your book next to the ISBN, and include the tagsn- in your book and website metadata.

The ability to control and edit the metadata for your book is a key reason you need to buy your own ISBN direct from Bowker and not to let someone else buy it for you.

TASKS FOR BUYING ISBNS

— Buy a block of 10 ISBN numbers from Bowker as described in Chapter 10: Get Your Book Into the System.

— When your book is ready to publish, log in to your account and fill out the metadata for your book.

— If you are creating a print book, then also buy a bar code.

5. Include metadata in documents and other media

Search engines take a peek inside all of the documents and applications you publish on the web for clues about its content. Almost all applications let you edit the metadata, though they might not call it metadata. For example, metadata resides in every Microsoft Word document you create and, if it's posted on the web, search engines will collect the author and company name (yours, or the owner of your bootlegged copy) to describe it. To edit the data in a Word document, simply open the document and click FILE > PROPERTIES to change or add the data.

If you're publishing audio, video, or any other media, make sure you edit the metadata inside that application, too. For example, Audacity, a free program handy for recording music, podcasts, and audiobooks, lets you insert ID3 tags that identify the recording to search engines and services like iTunes and Windows Media Player.

6. Include metadata on reseller sites

Ebook sites like Scribd, Issuu, and Smashwords, and online retailers like Amazon and Bn.com, want to distribute your book and allow their customers to discover and buy as many books as possible, which is why they make it easy for publishers to insert metadata. For example, if you've uploaded your ebook as a KDP file to Amazon, you will be prompted to insert the same kind of metadata as for the Bowker identifier services site.

7. Include metadata on social media sites

Never leave a profile field empty! Use all available information spaces on social media sites like Twitter, Facebook, LinkedIn, and YouTube to get found and create incoming links to your book's web presence. Any keyword-rich author bio you can place anywhere on the web (including at the end of guest blogs and articles) is valuable real estate. Facebook pages give you an opportunity to create even more metadata that creates incoming links to your website.

12

Create and Distribute Your Ebook

STEP 12
CREATE AND DISTRIBUTE YOUR EBOOK

With ebooks, your major concern is to get your book into the three formats that will reach the most readers: EPUB, Mobipocket/Amazon (Kindle) KDP, and PDF. Don't worry much about the others. During the slow evolution of ebooks many formats have been created and abandoned.

See Chapter 1: Choose a Publishing Path to determine what your ebook and POD strategies might be, and start publishing electronic versions of your work now. Here's how:

1. Pre-publish on social media and your website
2. Understand ebook formats
3. Understand platforms and hardware devices
4. Understand DRM protection
5. Understand sales and distribution channels
6. How to distribute to the major online retailers
7. Step-by-step to publishing your ebook

1. Pre-publish on social media and your website

Tools: Scribd, Facebook, your website (digital downloads,, e-store)

If you haven't already published teasers from your ebook on social publishing sites like Scribd, and created a Facebook author page, you should do that now, before you publish. It's not only a great way to develop your platform—your early readers can catch errors and give you input on your book before you go to all the time and expense of getting it formatted and distributed through more formal channels.

You can also start selling your text or PDF ebook directly from your own website before, and in conjunction with, distribution to online retailers. You or your webmaster will need to set up a PayPal account (preferably a merchant account) or otherwise incorporate a store into your website. (See Chapter 5 on websites for more information.)

When your book is perfect—edited, designed, proofed, and test marketed through the social publishing sites—then it's time to understand formats, choose a conversion process, and get your book distributed to the major ebook retailers.

2. Understand ebook formats

The major formats are EPUB, Amazon's KDP for Kindle (which is a DRM—Digitals Rights Management—version of Mobipocket), and PDF. Other important formats are Mobipocket, MSReader, Palm, HTML5, and text formats like doc, rtf, and txt.

Getting your book in EPUB, KDP, and PDF formats means your ebook can be aggregated to all the important devices and websites including Amazon, Google eBooks, Sony Reader, B&N NOOK, iPad and iPhone, and Android devices.

EPUB ebooks reach the most devices. EPUB is an open standard and most major device-makers deliver ebooks in this format. The EPUB format can accommodate images and other page design elements. EPUB fixed format, pioneered by Apple for the iPad, is an extension to EPUB that incorporates CSS to allow beautifully formatted books to be beautifully displayed in the device. EPUB is great for highly formatted publications. Tools: Smashwords, BookBaby, PubIt, BookBrewer, and more.

KDP (Kindle Direct Publishing) is Amazon's format for the Kindle platform, and is a DRM version of the Mobipocket format. Amazon-owned CreateSpace will create a KDP-formatted file for you for $65 when you publish a POD book with them. Tools: CreateSpace, MS Word.

PDF (Portable Document Format) is rigid, not reflowable, and is the format that you give to your printer to output the print book. A PDF-formatted ebook will look exactly like the print book and, unlike EPUB and other formats, does not allow text to reflow to fit the size of the device. (It is therefore not appropriate for small mobile devices.) Nevertheless, if you are already designing for print, you might as well offer an electronic PDF download for people who read them on larger devices and computer screens. Or, if your book is highly formatted, such as an art or photography book, PDF may be most appropriate. Tools: Adobe Acrobat Pro, InDesign, MS Word, any PDF conversion application.

The Mobipocket/AZW eReader is a DRM-free format for mobile devices, and LIT is the DRM-protected format for the Microsoft Reader. Tools: Smashwords, conversion service.

Don't forget text formats like doc (Word) format, txt and rtf. To get a step ahead in formatting your book, download one of Smashwords' book templates and use it when writing your book. When you're finished, it will be ready for sale and distribution in their store and to distribute to the major devices and in app stores. Tools: Smashwords.

HTML is also worth mentioning, as it is the format web browsers use, and it's also a step toward building a rich media book or app with embedded multimedia. Tools: Smashwords, website-building apps like Dreamweaver.

3. Understand platforms and hardware devices

E-reading devices are going through a drastic evolution. Many are single-purpose devices, which some experts expect will phase out in favor of multi-purpose devices like the iPad.

Here's how it works. To read a book on a device, the formatted ebook must be delivered to an e-reading platform, which may not be native to the device but is delivered via an app the user downloads. For example, the free Kobo app lets iPad/iPhone/ iPod Touch users read Kobo books (which the publisher delivered in EPUB format). iPad owners read Kindle books on the iPad by downloading the Kindle app.

By the way, Kindle is three things: a format, a hardware product/e-reading device, and a platform (or app). In the early days of ebooks, Kindle-formatted books could only be read on Amazon's Kindle e-reading device, but then they (and everybody else) got smart and created an app so customers could read their book on other devices. This means Amazon can sell Kindle books to people who want to read them on devices other than the Kindle e-reader, like the iPad.

Popular apps are Kindle, Kobo, Ibis Reader (HTML5 format), EPUB Reader for Firefox, Adobe Digital Editions, and Stanza (for Apple). There are more.

Popular e-reading devices are the Apple suite (iPad/iPhone/ iPod Touch), Amazon's Kindle, Android-powered mobile devices, any web browser (Firefox, IE, Safari), Sony eReader, NOOK, Kobo, and Google's iriver Story, to name a few.

4. Understand DRM protection

DRM stands for Digital Rights Management. Every author fears copyright infringement and piracy, but note that after a long, hard battle, the music industry no longer uses it. Not all ebook retailers are following suit, but DRM-free books are becoming the standard. However, when you format and distribute your book in EPUB for Apple, it will be wrapped in DRM. And the Amazon KDP format is a DRM-protected Mobipocket format. You don't have to worry about this as a separate step; the DRM is embedded in the formatting.

It is always illegal to pirate books and music, and to steal another person's writing, and instances are rarer than you think. Undiscovered self-published authors might even be happy to suddenly become widely pirated. If it happens, you can then take steps to correct it, and write a press release to let everyone know how popular you are.

5. Understand sales and distribution channels

A "channel" is a path through which you sell. If you upload your book for sale via Smashwords to distribute it to other ebook retailers, then Smashwords is one channel. If you upload your book individually to the Apple, Sony, and Amazon ebook stores, then you are selling via three channels. Add Scribd, ebook.com, and Barnes and Noble, and you've got six channels. Add your website, and that's seven. Each channel has its own requirements and contracts. None of them are exclusive, so you're free to use them all. Just don't cross-sell to a channel. For example, if you've already uploaded your ebook to Bn.com, do not ask Smashwords to distribute it there.

6. How to distribute to the major online retailers

If you've opted to use an ebook conversion service, they'll deliver the files to you. Once you have the files, visit the online retailer's website and look for the publishers' area where they will have specific instructions on how to join their program and upload your ebook for sale. You'll fill out the metadata for your book, specify how they should pay you, and click "I agree" to all of their terms.

7. Step-by-step to publishing your ebook

There are multiple paths to ebook publishing.

+ Pre-publish drafts or sample chapters to a browser-based social publishing site like Scribd for social media attention. Later, you might decide to use their ebook sales and distribution services but, like the Facebook author page, they really excel at social media marketing.

+ Format your book as needed to get onto the platforms and devices you think will work for you (as detailed in Chapter 1: Choose a Publishing Path).

+ If you've hired an ebook conversion service, upload your books individually to the various online retailers.

+ Upload your ebook to Google eBooks and promote it through their partner program. Also upload to any other online retailer you think will work for you.

+ Sell directly from your website using a digital downloads feature. Here's where coupon codes really pay off. (See also the chapters on social media and marketing and promotion.

Throughout the life of your book, ontinue to look for speciality websites and curators in your subject area for possible sales through their channels. For example, target your romance book to allromancebooks.com.

Speaking of ebooks, here's a special offer for you.
Scan the image below with your mobile phone's
QR Code Reader app to get details.

*Works with the i-nigma QR Code
Reader app and others.*

Create and
Distribute
Your Print Book

STEP 13
CREATE AND DISTRIBUTE YOUR PRINT BOOK

For those of us who want to print our books, there are almost too many choices. You can use a POD vendor to experiment with interior and exterior designs, plus galley proofs for final proofreading. Then you can print a short run of advance reading copies (ARCs) for reviewers. After you are sure the book is perfect, you may choose to continue using POD or short-run vendors to avoid holding inventory, or decide to invest in a large quantity of offset print books.

Authors of full-color books have fewer options because printing on demand is very, very expensive and the color quality is not as high as that done by offset print equipment. Some color book authors use POD author services companies to test design and concepts, and then use a print broker to find an offset printer, usually in Asia.

If you are publishing both a print book and an ebook, you may want to look for a vendor that does both. These include author services companies Blurb, Lulu, and CreateSpace, which print POD and distribute to ebook resellers. See Chapter 1: Choose a Publishing Path for more information. Whichever method you choose, here are your step-by-step guide and decision points.

1. Print your proof
2. Print ARCs for reviewers
3. Print on demand (POD)
4. Print a large quantity with an offset print vendor
5. Find a vendor who does it all

1. Print your proof

Your proof is for proofreading, so you will want to print just a few. If you've printed with an author services company, you will naturally order copies from them. If not, you will submit your trouble-free PDF cover and interior to a POD vendor according to their specifications. Small numbers of copies are much more expensive than short runs or offset print books, so you will want to try to minimize the number of proofs you print. Offset print vendors will probably charge you for proofs, in addition to their setup fees. Many first-time publishers print and correct many times, until they feel the book is right. It's a smart strategy, especially if you're sending ARCs to reviewers to create a platform and promote yourself and your book.

TIPS FOR GETTING PROOFS

— Order proof copies for careful review before printing a quantity of ARCs.

— Find recommendations for POD and short-run printers on the resources page.

— Make the changes you need to make. Repeat until perfect.

2. Create ARCs for reviewers

It's traditional to send book reviewers an ARC several months in advance of publication. You can print these books using a POD service that charges no up-front fees, or print a short run of 100 books with a service like 48HrBooks.

Bloggers and other casual reviewers might review your book immediately away, but if you want reviews in Foreword or other traditional channels, you'll need a four- to six-month lead time.

It's okay to send an imperfect book for review as long as it's marked "Publisher's Proof" or "Advance Reading Copy."

See Chapter 7: Market and Promote for how to develop media lists of people who might review your book.

Here's what you need to have on the front and back cover of the book if you're sending out ARCs. (Do this even if you are only sending elecrronic ARCs.)

ARC COVER CHECKLIST

— Make sure the cover is prominently marked with the disclaimer ADVANCE READING COPY. It should also be marked "Publisher's uncorrected proof—not for sale." If your cover art is not final (or close enough), you can create a separate, plain, single-color cover just for the advance copy.

— On the back cover, list the following information so that reviewers can reference this information in their book reviews:

Release date

Number of pages

Book size

Price

ISBN number

Marketing copy

— Put a notice on the back of the book that reads something like this:

PLEASE NOTE: This is an uncorrected proof. Any quotes for publication must be checked against the finished book. Price and publication date are subject to change without notice. Inquiries should be directed to Misadventures Media at 415.555.8888 or info@selfpubbootcamp.com.

3. Print on Demand (POD)

The big advantage to POD is that it is a low-cost and risk-free way to do business because you don't hold inventory. The downside is that it costs more per book to print on demand than it does to print a large quantity of books with an offset press (which prints higher-quality books).

Another advantage to POD with an author services company like CreateSpace, Blurb, and Lulu is that they may handle distribution to major distributors including Ingram, Baker & Taylor, Barnes and Noble, and Amazon.com, so you don't have to pay to ship the book from the printer to you, and then pay again to ship it to your distributor. Even large, mainstream publishers are opting to print their books on demand instead of holding inventory. See Chapter 1: Choose a Publishing Path for more information.

4. Print a large quantity with an offset print vendor

Offset print books are of higher quality and much cheaper per book than POD printing because of the machinery and quantity—most won't print fewer than 1,000 books at a time. Print brokers may be able to get you a very good deal on offset printing.

Authors with full-color, photography, and children's books are most likely to want to print high-quality books with an offset print vendor.

If your book is a standard trade paperback, and you know you can sell hundreds of books at events or through a particular venue, then it's very cost-effective to find an offset print vendor to print at least 1,000. You may sell the other 500 at events and from your website faster than you think. And don't forget the freebies you can send to important people for your promotion activities.

Offset printing can take six to eight weeks from order to delivery—more if you are printing a full-color book overseas. Don't forget to factor in the proof approval process. If you are printing a color book, you will definitely want to check that the four-color process results in the four colors you expected. So plan ahead.

Compose a Request for Quote (RFQ)

You can send out 100 RFQs and get 100 different price quotes. You may want to enlist the help of a print broker if you are printing a full-color book.

Use the checklist below, and you can copy the sample RFQ provided on the Self-Publishing Boot Camp website to prepare your own RFQ.

REQUEST FOR QUOTE CHECKLIST

— Your name, address, and contact information: For your printer and their shipping company.

— Your book specs: Size, number of pages, paper weight and color, recycled, soy ink, etc.

— The quantities you'd like quotes for (750; 1,000; 2,500; etc.).

— Cover lamination: Matte or glossy.

— Shrink wrapping: This helps keep books clean, and you can sell books in sixes or tens, too.

— Cover overruns: You want them. They're great for book displays.

— Delivery to a residence: Narrow streets, hills, alleyways may require delivery by small truck.

— Full bleeds on cover (probably) and interior (mostly for photography and art books).

— How you will deliver the files. For example: "PDF cover and interior created in Mac InDesign CS3."

Use a print broker

Enlist the help of a print broker—they know the market and which printer is likely to give you the best price. They will quote you print prices with their percentage already factored in. You may be surprised that, even with their cut, they can get lower prices than you can.

TIPS FOR FINDING A PRINT BROKER

— Search the web to find print brokers. Bookmarket.com has a good list of brokers. If you're a member of a publishing organization, they may have a list of recommended brokers.

— Talk to as many print brokers as it takes to find one you like and who likes you and your project.

— Ask for samples of books from the printers they represent and also for client referrals.

5. Find a vendor who does it all

More vendors than ever are now offering multiple printing services: POD, offset, digital short runs, and ebook printing and distribution. They may also have deals with major distribution channels that serve brick-and-mortar stores as well as online and ebook marketplaces.

You only have to upload your book file once, you have one representative to talk with, and you can concentrate on writing and promotion—the two things nobody else can do for you. Co- and partner-publishers like book packagers, distributors, printing companies, small presses, literary agents, and author services companies offer varying levels of service quality in this area.

14

Consider a Multimedia Book or App

STEP 14
CONSIDER A MULTIMEDIA BOOK
OR APP

First, some definitions. In a nutshell, an ebook is a digital snapshot of a book, an enhanced ebook adds multimedia and interactive features as interruptions to the linear story, and a book app is based on a book but acts more like a game with multiple pathways that require the user to interact instead of simply scrolling and clicking.

Common additions to a transmedia book are an author introduction, video clips, and hyperlinks to information on the internet. A transmedia book may also be referred to as an enhanced or rich media book, book mashup, enriched, hybrid, v-book, Vook, or amplified book. Transmedia books can be created in a book page layout program like InDesign, and require the skills of a book or web designer.

A book app can do everything an enhanced ebook does but crosses the line from linear storytelling to non-linear storytelling, allowing the user to choose from multiple pathways and to select from a potentially huge number of photos, videos, audio files, illustrations, hyperlinks, and interactivity. Apps are third-party software programs requiring the skills of a programmer with C++ or Apple's Objective C programming knowledge.

Much confusion arises from the fact that so many books are bundled as apps so they can be sold in an app store. There are more ebooks than games in the iPhone App Store, and it's rumored that Apple may purge such ebooks as they have purged other overly simple apps. It might be argued that there is little point to ebook app-wrapping when compared with more elegant, library-based ebook stores and their e-reader apps (the iBookstore download to the iBook e-reader app, for example), which give customers a more consistent user experience and keeps the device desktop uncluttered. However, authors want it, so services are providing it.

The transmedia ebook and app space is still very experimental, but expect industry standards to emerge and the market to adjust to the technical possibilities.

1. How to create a transmedia book

2. How to create a book-based mobile app

1. How to create a transmedia book

You can use the InDesign book layout program—or hire a designer—to create a simple or complex transmedia book with embedded audio and video files, hyperlinks and anchor links, and animated graphics.

The media and interactivity may include music, audio, video, slideshows, news feeds, illustrations, and background materials. You may also provide searchable text, tilt scrolling, internal and external links, and Flash animations into the linear story. Creating an enhanced ebook requires the skills of a book designer or web developer.

Many publishers make the mistake of adding multimedia to an ebook just because they have it. This can be a mistake because many readers like the immersive quality of the reading process, and interruptions can distract and irritate. So plan carefully and do some user testing. If you're writing a non-fiction book about music history, readers may appreciate music samples in key areas of the book. Avoid self-congratulatory author-based material.

Your book designer simply needs the multimedia files you want to include, and direction on where to embed them to output a PDF-formatted transmedia book. To create a transmedia book in the EPUB format, look for web designers, book designers, and formatters looking to expand their repertoires. Everybody's on a learning curve.

2. How to create a book-based mobile app

When you've got so much material that linear storytelling is no longer practical, it might be time to consider an app as an add-on product to your book. Children's books are especially ripe for apps and complement the ebook edition. Game-type apps are the most complex and dense with media and multiple user choices, or paths. Other book-related apps you may want to consider include card decks, calendars, and spoken-word apps.

There are several ways to go about creating an app:

— Recruit an app development and publishing firm.

— Hire a C++ programmer to develop the app for you.

— Find a DIY app generator that suits your needs.

A professional app development company employs a team that includes C++/Objective C programmers, graphic designers, professional actors and custom narration, music soundtrack and sound effects, interactivity specialists, editors, and page layout designers for the different devices. The price tag for a complex, quality book-based app is in the five-figures. But if your book app idea is compelling enough, you may be able to recruit one of these firms to partner with you for a royalty.

You could hire a C++ programmer to build your app for you. But make sure that person is familiar with the kind of business you're in and your audience. The developer should have multimedia and web development skills, too, in order to understand, imagine, contribute, and help you succeed with a marketable app. Before hiring, as always, get samples and recommendations, and make sure you get along. The relationship will likely be tested during the creative development process.

Finally, there are the do-it-yourself options, and they are popping up quickly. For example, travel guidebook authors are flocking to Sutro Media, a company who developed a browser-based tool to let authors easily upload material to a content management system. The material is then ported into Objective C on the back end to create the app. These apps allow the authors to include all the photos they had to leave out of their book versions, and include live maps and hyperlinks, too.

Sutro does not require the author to pay any upfront costs, but they carefully evaluate proposed projects. Their payment model is a revenue-sharing agreement with a royalty split of 30% each going to Sutro, Apple, and the author, with the remaining 10% going to their in-house editor.

Today's DIY mobile app market is confusing and crowded with app generators that do simple things like create an app that streams your RSS feed (from your blog, for example) and create coupons. It's difficult to find a good DIY mobile app builder suitable for book-based apps.

As always, look to the Self-Publishing Boot Camp resources page for up-to-date information.

Resources

RESOURCES

On the Web

Check out the SelfPubBootCamp.com website for an ever-growing list of resources and recommendations to products and services we trust, including book designers, photographers, editors, website hosting, printers, business books, and book packagers.

Workshops and Conferences

Check the calendar for upcoming Self-Publishing Boot Camp workshops, conferences, and appearances. Contact us about booking a workshop in your area, about speaking to your group, class, conference, or about developing a custom workshop to fit your needs.

Join the Discussion Online

SelfPubBootCamp is on Facebook and Twitter. Follow for information and trends, recommendations, and conversations about the self-publishing process.

Other Services

Self-Publishing Boot Camp offers speaking, consulting, custom books, conference content, and educational materials. For more information please contacr us via the SelfPubBootCamp.com website contact form to be sure your request does not get lost in a spam filter. Thank you!

Misadventures Media

13424766R00090

Made in the USA
Charleston, SC
10 July 2012